The Best Man's Speech

The Best Man's Speech

A tough job made easy

from **confetti.co.uk**
don't get married without us...

First published in 2004
by Octopus Publishing Group
2–4 Heron Quays
London E14 4JP
www.conran-octopus.co.uk
Reprinted in 2004 (twice), 2005

Written for Confetti by Sticky Content Ltd
Text copyright © 2004 Confetti Network Ltd;
Book design and layout copyright © 2004
Conran Octopus Ltd;
Illustrations copyright © 2004 Confetti Network Ltd

A catalogue record for this book is available from
the British Library.
ISBN 1 84091 369 X

Publishing Director Lorraine Dickey
Senior Editor Katey Day
Assistant Editor Sybella Marlow
Art Director Chi Lam
Designer Jeremy Tilston
Assistant Production Controller Natalie Moore

Other books in this series include *How to Write a Wedding
Speech*; *Jokes, Toasts and One-liners for Wedding Speeches*;
The Best Man's Wedding; *Wedding Readings*; *Speeches*;
Men at Weddings and *The Wedding Book of Calm*.

Contents

The best man's speech

People love wedding speeches – they look forward to them, listen to them, discuss them, remember them. The best man's speech is often the most eagerly anticipated and attentively listened to of all. So it's not surprising that making the speech has become the centrepiece of the best man's role and is likely to dominate the way in which you prepare for the big day.

Before you get too stressed at the prospect, put your speech into perspective. True, you'll be the centre of attention for five minutes or so, but the day really belongs to the couple, and most of the time everyone will be focusing on them. The trick is to make your five minutes really count.

A best man's speech should be something that all the guests remember for the right reasons – because it's entertaining, funny, touching, considerate and does everything that it's supposed to. This might seem like a tall order if you're not practised in the art of public speaking, but with the right approach and lots of preparation you can do it.

Packed with practical advice, useful information and loads of sample material, this book is here to help.

In accordance with tradition...

Of course you'll want to make your speech as entertaining as possible, but traditionally the best man's speech is also expected to cover certain points and fulfil certain functions.

Traditionally, for instance, the best man will...

• Introduce all the other speakers, unless there is a toastmaster. Nowadays, speakers can be quite numerous as more people often choose to speak.
• Read any messages from friends and family who haven't been able to attend.
• Propose a toast to the bride and groom.

Your speech will also be expected to include...

• Thanks to the groom for his toast to the bridesmaids.
• Comments on the happy couple, particularly the groom.
• Comments on how great the day has been.
• Thanks to the organizers.

Your role, in short, is a multiple one. As the groom's best friend, you will be expected to subject him to an ordeal of gentle embarrassment. As host, you will read out telegrams and pass on any practical announcements. And as traditional head of the wedding assistants, you will also speak on behalf of the bridesmaids.

Last but not least

Speeches are traditionally given in a certain order:

• Father of the bride
• Groom
• Best man

It's becoming more usual for other people to make a speech, too – the mother of the bride and chief bridesmaid, for example, may also want to say a few words. But however many people speak, the best man traditionally always goes last – saving the best till then, hopefully.

Good timing

Speeches are usually made after the main meal, so by the time the best man comes to make his, the guests tend to have relaxed considerably (a fact not unconnected with the wine that will be disappearing from the tables). This can often work in your favour, as by now, the guests will be nicely warmed up and well disposed to laugh at your jokes.

However, this can also mean that you end up spending the meal feeling nervous – or worse, over-indulging in the name of Dutch courage. A drink or two may help steady your nerves, but don't overdo it: a slurred speech will be remembered for all the wrong reasons!

Just relax...

While it's easy to get completely absorbed in making your speech and forget about your other duties as best man, it's not in the interests of either your speech or your relationship with the groom to do so.

Organizing the ushers, introducing guests to one another and generally making sure everything runs smoothly are all part of your job. If you concentrate on doing these things, you'll not only be fulfiling your role properly, but you'll also be distracting yourself from any pre-speech nerves.

Remember that you weren't asked to be best man because of your ability to rattle off gags like a stand-up comedian. The best man is chosen because he's the groom's best friend and he wouldn't have picked you if he didn't think you could do the job. So just relax, take it easy and let your natural wit shine through.

Your wedding speech toolkit

This section is a practical guide to everything you'll need in order to put together a winning speech.

Preparation is where it all begins, so we open up the many available avenues of research to help you start compiling and building on your speech material. That material needs to be suitable, of course, so make sure that your words don't start a fight or upset granny. We look in detail at what to keep and what to chuck. Remember: if in doubt, leave it out!

Timing, delivery, pace… as every stand-up knows, how you say it is just as important – perhaps even more important – than what you say. From eye contact to stage fright, we advise on how to deliver like a pro.

Your wedding speech toolkit also covers some of the more daring weapons in the best man's armoury, such as comedy props and speech games.

Preparing your speech

Preparation is at the heart of a good speech. Scribbling down a few words the night before the big day is not going to work. Keep your speech on the back burner of your brain as soon as you know you are going to be best man, and start really working on it a few weeks before the wedding.

It's an unfailing rule: the more prepared you are, the more confident you will be about giving your speech, and the more your audience will enjoy it. And the more you'll enjoy it, too.

Remember that your speech will be expected to include:
• Thanks to the groom for his toast on behalf of the bridesmaids and for any gifts that were presented.
• Comments on the bride and groom – you could mention how great they look today or why they're so compatible.
• Compliments to the groom. Brides always get a lot of attention at weddings, and your speech is a good chance to redress the balance a little.
• Amusing anecdotes about the groom's misdemeanours in the past and/or jokes at the groom's expense.

Putting it all together

Decide what kind of speech you want to make before you start putting it together. You could:

• Make a speech on your own.

• Make a joint speech with the ushers, other friends or the chief bridesmaid.

• Perform a stunt and/or use props.

• Use a home video or slides or invent funny telegrams.

• Adopt a well-known format to comic effect. For example, you could write a mock school report for the bride/groom and base your jokes around that.

Don't think about your speech as one big lump. Break it down into headings and decide what you're going to say under each one – for instance, how you met the groom, wedding preparations, how the bride and groom got to know each other. Then look at all the elements and work out the best order to fit them together.

As you prepare, make sure you have:

• A notebook so you can start jotting down ideas as they occur to you.

• A tape recorder so you can practise and time your speech.

• Friends and family to listen to your speech and give you ideas.

• Any necessary props.

• A copy of the latest draft of your speech to carry round with you, so you can make notes and work on it whenever you have a spare moment.

Revealing sources

Good research can turn a mildly amusing speech into an uproariously funny one. Nothing can beat that cringe-inducing anecdote or photo from the groom's early years that you have managed to excavate and that he was clearly hoping no one could possibly remember – and may even have forgotten about himself.

As best man you probably know the groom very well, but you may not know much about his family life or early schooldays – times people enjoy hearing anecdotes about. So start your research early so that you have time to gather everything you need.

Friends united

The best sources of stories about a bride and groom are, of course, their friends and family. Siblings, cousins, mates and colleagues probably all have some great anecdotes to tell. As soon as you know you're doing a speech, send out emails asking people who know the happy couple for any funny/touching stories they think you could include. Or invite everyone out for a drink, bring your tape recorder along and let them reminisce away. You're sure to come away with some great material.

Every picture tells a story

Photograph albums are a great source of speech material, too. Old pictures, or the stories behind them, can be hilarious. If there's a snap of the groom or bride pulling a face in a school photo or looking cute as a toddler, get it blown up to display on the night and work it into the speech.

For instance, a picture of the groom as a five-year-old enjoying a donkey ride at the seaside can be used as an illustration of his lifelong affection for the gee-gees, while a snap of him as a naked tot at bathtime can show how much he's always loved water sports, for example.

Not everyone at the wedding will have known the bride and groom for long. Using photographs of them as tiny children can help to bridge the gap between friends and family. It also gives you licence to comment on their childhood hobbies, eccentricities, fashion sense, etc and make comical comparisons with the grown-up people they are today.

What the papers say

Are there any newspaper cuttings about the happy couple? Perhaps he appeared in the local paper in his days as top goal scorer for the under-nines football team, or she was a prize-winning Girl Guide. You could use this type of material to illustrate how much they've changed... or how much they haven't, as the case may be.

You could also look at the news for the year the groom was born and work it into your speech. For example: '1969 was the year Neil Armstrong took a small step for man and a giant leap for mankind by walking on the moon, and coincidentally, it was also the year Paul took his first steps...' If you can find a photograph of the groom and incorporate it into your speech, so much the better.

PCs can be used to great effect to create front page newspaper mock-ups: you could use a *Sun* headline such as 'Gotcha' to accompany a picture of the couple getting engaged. Get the picture blown up as large as possible and display it while you're making your speech.

Written in the stars

Zodiac signs make for great speech fodder. Use them to compare the characteristics/vices of the sign the groom was born under to the way he actually is. If, for instance, his star sign says he's generous and brave, but in fact he's notoriously thrifty and a bit of a coward, you're well away.

For example: 'Geminis are meant to be communicative and witty, with a reputation for being the life and soul of the party. Well, I guess that's one way of describing James on his stag night…' Or: 'Richard's such a quiet, gentle guy that many people don't realize he's a Leo, which is, of course, a fire sign. But I can assure you that, as far as Helen is concerned, he's burning up with passion.'

Books that discuss star sign compatibility can also provide some funny lines for speeches, as can reading out the horoscope for the day. It doesn't need to be a real one – just make up something to suit the occasion, for example: 'My horoscope says today is a day for pure relaxation – wonder what went wrong there then?'

By any other name...

There's often mileage in the meaning of the names of the bride or groom: 'Apparently, the name Gary means "spear carrier". Well, I don't know about a spear but he certainly carries a torch for Kathleen.' You could also compare the meanings of the couple's names.

Stars in their eyes

Think of a famous person with whom the bride or groom shares a name and compare them in terms of image, job, clothes, etc. For example, 'Tom Cruise may have made his millions and worked with most of Hollywood's major directors, while our Tom has made a few quid and enjoys a pint of Directors. However, I think he's the more fortunate guy, as Tom Cruise didn't have much luck with Nicole, but our Tom has got Isabel, and their love is something money and fame can't buy.'

Whatever they like...

You don't have to stick to jokes about football teams – hobbies and interests of all kinds can form the basis of lots of stories. However, you might not be as familiar with the groom's obsessions as he is. In this case, the internet is a great source of information.

If one of the happy couple is a huge fan of any singer or celebrity and their obsession is well known, you could use it in your speech. For example: 'Roger has always been a major Elvis fan, and when he met Rachel he was certainly All Shook Up. He almost moved into Heartbreak Hotel when he thought she wasn't interested...'

Make it work

Working life and old bosses can be a source of great material. If you're not a colleague of the bride or groom, get in touch with their workmates past and present and ask them for any good office anecdotes. Just make sure they're not too in-jokey so that everyone will understand them.

Ha ha ha

Jokes, jokes, jokes – every best man wants them. As well as your own jokes, renting comedy videos and films, asking people for their favourite gags and looking for funny lines on the internet can also provide you with inspiration.

If you do borrow jokes, you will need to personalize them to make them appropriate, rather than just throw them into the speech. The following sections of this book are full of examples of how to do this. Go for quality rather than quantity: a handful of well-polished witticisms will do you better service than a scatter-gun approach involving a hundred ill-digested one-liners.

Academic archive

Old schoolbooks, school reports and university notes can also provide material. Ask one of the groom's family to get them down from the attic and take a look. If there's a school report saying how your high-flying friend and groom will never amount to a hill of beans, or a funny essay they wrote when they were ten, it could be amusing to read it out.

Hands-on help

If you're worried about any aspect of your speech, talk it through with someone who's been there before. Talking to someone with experience will calm your nerves and give your confidence a boost. They survived the ordeal, after all! And if they still have a copy of their speech, ask to see it. They can also advise on how to source material, where they got their ideas from and how they put the whole thing together.

You can also learn from their mistakes, rather than making your own. They may have unwittingly stumbled on a sensitive subject, for example, or their speech may have overrun or been too short. Ask them which were the bits that really worked, and what were the things that could, in retrospect, have been improved on. Finding out how not to do it can be a great help in making your own effort a success. And if they are willing, ask them to read your speech after you've written it, for some last-minute expert advice.

The right material

Wedding speakers have it tough. Who else has to make a speech that will appeal to an audience with an age range of 2 to 82? Speeches have to make people laugh without offending anyone's sensibilities, talk about families and relationships without treading on anyone's toes and hold people's attention without stealing the show from the happy couple.

It sounds like a tall order, but most of the pitfalls of speech-making can be avoided if you know what to talk about and recognize that there are limits around certain subjects. It's all a matter of choosing and using your material with care.

Definite no-nos
You can get away with talking about a lot of subjects, provided you're genuinely witty and don't cross the line into bad taste. Some things, however, are absolutely off-limits. Steer clear of these topics:
• Race
• Religion
• Ex-partners
• People who refused to attend
• Last-minute threats to call off the wedding
• Swearing
• Explicit sexual references

Criticism

Weddings aren't the place for criticism. Don't knock anything relating to the venue or the service, and don't make jokes at other people's expense, especially the bride's. This is the happy couple's perfect day, and you need to help keep it that way by considering other people's feelings at all times.

Past romances

There's nothing wrong with talking about the groom's previous loves – provided they're really firmly in the far distant past.

Tell guests about the flirtation he had with that cute little blonde… in the sandpit back at nursery school.

Don't tell them about the girl who broke his heart when he was 16 and whom he's never really forgotten – or about any other romance he's had since the age of seven, for that matter. It's also worth noting that while you can make vague allusions to the groom's sowing of wild oats – such as 'He was a bit of a wild lad at college' – you should never even hint at anything similar about the bride. Double standards still apply, at least at weddings!

The happy couple's relationship

Comments about the bride and groom are usually part of the best man's speech. Tread carefully, however, especially if their relationship has been stormy in the past.

Tell guests about how their first meeting generated enough electricity to power the National Grid. Talk about how compatible they are and how great they both look today.

Don't tell them about how they slept together within half-an-hour of meeting or about how she left him for someone else for six months. Arguments, estrangements and threats to call off the wedding are all off limits.

If in any doubt, leave it out.

Bit of a lad

People expect funny stories about the groom's misdemeanours to be part of the best man's speech. Joshing him gently is all part of the fun, but do make sure that your anecdotes are humorous rather than offensive.

Tell guests about the time he redecorated the living room with crayon when he was a little lad.

Don't tell them about how he was all over that lap dancer at his stag night, then vomited copiously in the minicab all the way home. Keep quiet about criminal records, expulsions from school and the like, too.

Family matters

Complimenting the bride and groom's families can be part of your speech – but make sure you stick to compliments only. **Tell guests** how your best friend, the groom, has great parents – and now he's gaining great parents-in-law, as well as a lovely wife. Or congratulate the bride's parents for organizing the wedding so well.

Don't tell them how you're amazed to see the groom's father there at all since he scarpered when the groom was still in his pram. Speeches shouldn't be used for settling scores. Avoid comments about divorced or warring parents. If the family situation is very sensitive, resist the temptation to think you can make things better with a few carefully chosen lines.

The bride

It's possible that you may have ambivalent feelings about the bride. Keep these firmly under wraps at the wedding. Don't make any jokey remarks about her diet either! Compliments to the bride are the only permissible references to her in your speech.

Be kind

Sure, your speech is about teasing the groom, but mix the mockery with some sincerity. Talk about how highly you think of him, what a good friend he is and how his relationship with the bride has enriched him. Give the couple all your very best wishes for the future.

The wedding

Behind-the-scenes stories about preparing for the wedding, especially amusing incidents and narrowly averted disasters, make good ingredients for speeches. However, you might be surprised at how sensitive these subjects can be. No family exists who doesn't squabble over wedding arrangements. Sometimes these disagreements seem amusing by the time the big day arrives – but sometimes they don't, so take care. **Tell guests** how fantastically the day has turned out and how it's all down to the hard work of *all* the organizers. **Don't tell them** about how the bride's mother almost had a nervous breakdown over the seating plan – unless you're absolutely sure she'll think it's funny. As always, run your speech by someone close to the family first.

In-jokes

Making everyone feel included is one of the jobs of the best man. To make sure no one feels left out, think of all the people who might be listening when you write your speech. You need to explain references that not everyone may be familiar with, and if this takes too long, it's better to think of another anecdote.

Tell guests about how, one year, the groom broke three dozen eggs in the school egg and spoon race.

Don't tell them about that hilarious time in metalwork when the groom got told off by that mad Mr Smith, you know, the metalwork teacher, he was really mad, and he sent him to see Miss Green, the one who all the lads fancied... you really had to be there.

Tailored to fit

The material that you decide is suitable for your speech will depend on your audience. It's up to you to find out who you'll be talking to, and to check beforehand that what you want to say won't cause offence. If you can rehearse your speech in front of your mum and granny without them feeling uncomfortable or you feeling embarrassed, you're probably on to a winner.

Delivery

It ain't what you do...

As anyone who's made a successful speech will tell you, it's not what you say, it's the way you say it. And, as best man, you want to make sure the way you deliver and present your speech does justice to your carefully chosen material. Here's how.

Practice makes perfect

Reading your speech out again and again before the big day is essential if you want to perfect your delivery, make sure your material is suitable – and find out if your jokes are funny. Your speech should appeal to everyone, from your friends to your maiden aunt, so try to rehearse in front of a variety of people. Test it out on people who will give honest, constructive feedback. They will also be able to tell you when you're mumbling, or rambling, or just going on too long. You should also record your rehearsals on tape. That way, you will be able to review yourself and see where there's room for improvement and how you are for time – aim for five minutes as a rough guide.

The run-up

Your speech comes last, so you're going to spend some of the reception waiting to 'go on'. How you fill your time will affect your delivery.

Don't overindulge

Although it's very tempting to down a few too many glasses while you're waiting to speak – don't. Being tipsy could affect your delivery by making you slur your words and cause you to be unsteady on your feet. Too many drinks might also lead you to decide that the risqué story about what the groom got up to at the rugby club night out, which you deleted from your original speech, really should be in there after all.

Listen and learn

Listening to the other speeches will help take your mind off your nerves and help put you into the fun mood. Having a few laughs will relax you and make the time pass more quickly until, before you know it, it's your turn.

Have a banana

Many professional performers swear by the trick of eating a banana about 20 minutes before they start speaking. Doing this, they say, will give you a quick energy boost and help steady your nerves.

You're on!

Start right

Don't try to begin your speech when there are lots of
distractions. Wait until the audience has stopped applauding
the previous speaker, the tables have been cleared, the coffee
poured and everyone has settled so that you have people's
undivided attention.

Rambling prohibited

Timing is crucial when it comes to speeches. However
brilliant yours is, and however good a speaker you are,
five minutes is more than enough. People enjoy listening
to speeches, true, but they want to get on with talking
and dancing, too, so keep it short. Rambling speeches are a
mistake. Make sure yours has a firm beginning, middle and
end. Steer clear of shaggy dog stories in favour of short,
pithy jokes and asides. When it comes to speeches, less is
definitely more.

Eye to eye

Make eye contact when you're making your speech – just
not with everyone at once! Speak as if you were talking to
one person and focus on them. You can look around the
room if you want to, but focus on one person at a time. The
trick is to imagine that you're simply chatting to someone.

Don't look down

Even if you decide to learn your speech off by heart, you will need to have some notes to refer to in case your mind goes blank in the heat of the moment. However, don't deliver your speech while hiding behind a quivering piece of paper or constantly staring downwards. Look down for a moment, look up and speak. Get into a rhythm of doing this throughout your speech.

No mumbling

When people get nervous, they tend to swallow their words; this can render a beautifully written speech nearly inaudible. You don't want to deliver your speech only to find that no one could actually hear what you were saying, so check that you're audible by arranging beforehand for someone at the back of the room to signal when your voice isn't carrying.

Breathtaking

Another way to combat the mumbling menace is by breathing properly. Take deep, rhythmic breaths. This will pump oxygen into your blood and keep your brain sharp and alert.

Set the pace

Gabbling is another thing people tend to do when they're nervous. To stop yourself talking too fast, write the word 'pause' at intervals through your notes, or if you are using cue cards, insert blank ones that will automatically cause you to slow down. If you do lose your place, it's best just to make a joke of it.

Move on swiftly

Pause briefly after you make a joke to give people a chance to laugh, but keep jokes and anecdotes short so that if one doesn't work, you can move on quickly to the next. If your joke dies, don't despair. Turn the situation to your advantage by inserting a quip such as 'Only me on that one then', or look round at an imaginary assistant and say: 'Start the car!' 'Rescue lines' like these can earn you a chuckle from a momentarily awkward silence.

Keep smiling

Being best man and making a speech are supposed to be fun, so make sure you don't look utterly miserable when you're doing it. Smile! Think of something that makes you laugh before you start speaking to get yourself into the fun mood. Body language is important, too, so adopt a relaxed posture before you begin – no crossed arms or fidgeting.

Stage fright

It's only natural to be nervous. If you find that you're really scared when you begin, don't panic. Make a joke out of it instead. Lines like 'This speech is brought to you in association with Imodium' or 'I was intending to speak but my tongue seems to be welded to the roof of my mouth' should raise a laugh and will help to get the audience on your side. One completely bald best man started off on a high note by remarking: 'As you can see, I've been so worried about making this speech, I've been tearing my hair out.' There's no shame in admitting you're a wee bit scared.

Start strongly

Opening lines are important, because they grab the audience's attention and get you off to a good start. Something like: 'Ladies and gentlemen, they say speeches are meant to be short and sweet, so thank you and good night,' should help you to begin in style.

All in the mind

Instead of seeing your speech as a formal ordeal, think of it as being a conversation between you and a lot of people you know and really like, or as a way of wishing two good friends well. Thinking positively about your speech and the reason why you are there will help you to deliver it with confidence and make the task seem less intimidating.

To help calm your nerves beforehand, imagine your speech being over and everyone applauding. Imagine how you'll feel when you can sit down and relax, knowing that the moment is over and you can now really enjoy the rest of the evening. By visualizing everything going well, this will help to give you even more confidence.

They're on your side

Remember that weddings are happy occasions and all the guests want to see everything go well, including your speech. Be assured, the audience is on your side, they're all rooting for you, so make the most of it and use their goodwill to boost your confidence.

Give it meaning

Think about the meaning of your speech while you're making it. Concentrate on the thoughts you want to convey and the message behind your words, rather than just reciting your notes, as this will help you to make your delivery more expressive.

Round it off

End your speech with a toast. This will give it a focus and provide something to work towards. After you make your toast, you can sit down when everyone else sits down, signifying a definite end to your speech. Our range of sample toasts starts on page 114.

Using prompts and props

Memory joggers

Reading an entire speech from a sheet of paper can make it sound a bit lifeless and can stop you from making eye contact with the audience. One way to get around this is to memorize your speech and use prompts to remind you of what to say.

To cut down on the amount of text you use, first write the speech out, then make very brief notes that remind you of each part of it. Gradually cut back on your text, so the notes say as much as you need to jog your memory.

On cue

Make a set of cue cards. These are small index cards with key phrases that remind you of different parts of your speech, stacked in the order that you say them. Inserting blank cards for pauses can help you pace your speech. Even if you feel you need to put your whole speech on cards, they are still preferable to a piece of paper, because you will need to pause and look up as you turn them.

Proper props

Physical gags, games, visuals and tricks can all be part of
a best man's speech. So if you don't want to be stuck just
reading a prepared text – don't be. Let your imagination
run wild.

If your speech is going to involve the use of props, make sure
that you do plenty of rehearsing with them beforehand, and
also ensure that any machinery is in good working order
before the big day.

Make 'em look

Simple props can be used to begin with a bang. One best
man, for instance, started off his speech with the remark:
'I hate it when people use cheap gimmicks to get attention,
don't you?' before whipping off his baseball cap and pony
tail to reveal a completely bald pate.

Lots of different props can be used for this type of joke.
Why not try:
• A revolving bow tie
• Clown feet
• A whistle
• A clown nose?

Great gags

Little trike

One motorcycle-mad groom thought he'd do something really different on his wedding day by roaring into the reception on his brand-new Harley Davidson. Only, unknown to him, his younger brother-cum-best man had got wind of the plan. As the groom arrived at the top table on his gleaming steed, he heard a strange creaking noise coming from the back of the room. He turned around to see his brother upstage him completely by trailing behind on a rusty child's tricycle.

Mopping up

Harry and Sam are a pair of brothers known for their sensitivity, so when Harry got married it wasn't surprising that both he and best man Sam were in floods of tears before the speeches had even started. But when the time came for Harry to be Sam's best man, he decided to come prepared. Before beginning his speech, he produced an enormous plastic bag stuffed with packets of tissues, which he distributed among the audience. It wasn't long before they were throwing them back at him.

Picture perfect

When he was best man for his friend Pete, Richard decided to use a flip chart of photographs and a pointer to liven up his speech. Only the pictures weren't ones of the happy couple as toddlers or newspaper cuttings of their achievements. Instead there was a skip – representing Pete's first car; a picture of a bombsite – representing his bedroom; and so on. It was a simple idea, but it got big laughs.

Loud and clear

A quick visual gag can get a speech off to a great start, as Michael demonstrated when he was best man. When he started speaking the audience couldn't hear a word because he was mumbling so much – until he produced a huge loudhailer and roared 'Can you hear me at the back?' through it.

Read the signs

Introduce your speech by saying that you've got a sore throat and can't speak very loudly, so your friend is going to use sign language to interpret what you're saying. Your friend will then make exaggerated and ridiculous hand gestures to accompany your speech. Obviously, this one will need a lot of rehearsal.

Hat trick

Have a series of funny hats under the table that you put on as you run through the groom's life story – for example a baby bonnet, a school cap, a mortar board, a fireman's helmet, a baseball cap, a deerstalker. The more ridiculous the hats, the better.

Good report

Write a mock school report on the bride or groom and read it out, relating it to the events of the day, such as: 'It says here that Paula doesn't suffer fools gladly... which is bad news as she's just got married to Steve.'

Video diary

Get your friends together and make a spoof video documentary featuring their thoughts and feelings about the bride and groom. A couple could dress up as the happy couple and re-enact their first meeting.

Games to play
Playing speech games is a way of getting the whole audience to join in the fun. Try:

The singing game
Ask friends and family to help compile a list of words that describe the guests at each table. Put the lists on the respective tables and ask everyone sitting at them to make up a song or poem using all of the words on the list. They then have to stand up and perform it!

The limerick game
This is another word game that everyone can enjoy. You put a note on all the tables asking the guests to make up a short poem or limerick about the couple. You can read out the best ones during your speech, or ask the guests to read out their own. Make it clear however, that you don't want anything offensive.

The sweepstake game
At the start of the reception, get the ushers to ask guests to bet on the length of the speeches. The person who makes the closest guess wins the total amount, either to keep or to donate to a charity of their choice.

The key game

This is a favourite among wedding speechmakers as it really helps to break the ice. To play it, you need to get in touch with all the female guests beforehand (you might have to hang around the ladies at the reception to do it) and fill them in on the plan.

During your speech you then say something like: 'Neil has got what you might call a chequered past, but now that he's married to Hannah it's time that he began afresh. So I'm asking any of his ex-girlfriends who may be present to give back the keys to his flat. Just come up here and put them in this bowl. Come on girls, don't be shy.'

Then, you've guessed it, all the women at the reception, from the groom's 90-year-old auntie to his four-year-old cousin will come up to put a set of keys in the bowl. It's guaranteed to get laughs and helps everyone to relax.

Pass the parcel

Present the bride with an enormous parcel. As she unwraps it, it gets smaller and smaller until she comes to a little box. In it, there's a note saying 'I haven't got much to say, but thanks for padding out my speech.'

Instant nostalgia

Props don't have to be used for jokes. You could put together video, photographs and newspaper cuttings to make a quick 'this is your life' of the bride and groom, or have a blast from the past by playing a tape of the band the groom used to be in.

As with speeches, so with props. You should never attempt to wing it when making a speech, but this is even more important when using props. Make sure that you rehearse well and run your idea by other members of the wedding party to reduce the risk of your joke falling flat.

Wedding speech checklist

Once you've agreed to speak

No matter how much warning you've had of your best mate's upcoming nuptials and your role on the big day, the success of your speech will ultimately result from the amount of prep you've put in. So as soon as you accept the job of best man...

• Start thinking about research.

• Think about the audience. Your speech will have to appeal to a wide range of people, from great aunt Nora to your friends from work.

• It's your job to find out who'll be among the guests so that your material appeals and you don't cause offence.

• Ask friends and family for funny stories/embarrassing pictures that you can build into your speech.

• Keep your speech in the back of your mind. You never know when you might pick up a titbit of information or some juicy material.

• Keep a notebook to hand. Great ideas often strike when you least expect them (like on the train or in the bath!).

• Speak to someone who's been a best man and find out what not to do.

• Decide on the kind of speech you want. Will you need any props or visual aids or any equipment?

The build-up

A few weeks before the big day, start working on your speech in earnest.

• Think about the structure. Would the speech be better broken down into manageable chunks/themes?

• Does your speech do what it's supposed to do? Is it funny, affectionate and charming without being offensive?

• Have you included everything you need to in your speech? thanks to the groom for his toast to the bridesmaids, thanks to the organizers, etc.

• Find out who else will be making a speech. Nowadays the list of people who want to say a few words can be quite long and, unless there is a toastmaster, it will fall to you to introduce all the other speakers.

• Gather all the props/presentation aids you'll need and make sure you know how to use them.

• Build in time to practise your speech – the better rehearsed you are, the more confident you'll be, and the more everyone will enjoy it, yourself included.

Only a week to go

A week or so before the big day, start honing down
your speech.

- Use a tape recorder or video to record yourself.
- Rope in an audience of friends to practise on.
- Be sure to practise your speech with any props you plan
to use – winging it on the day is not a good bet.
- Time your speech. Aim to keep it to around five minutes.
Brevity really is the soul of wit.
- Don't forget to allow time for reading out messages from
absent friends and family, passing on practical announcements
and so on.
- Write your speech in note form on cue cards, even if you
intend to commit it to memory.
- Think positively about your speech and it will feel like less
of an ordeal.
- Visualize your speech being over and everyone applauding
as it will help to give you confidence and calm your nerves.
- Remember the audience is on your side – you'll be able to
use their goodwill to boost your confidence.

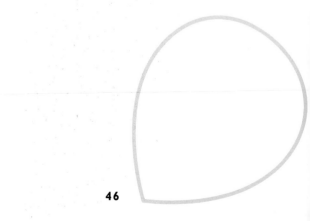

The big day

As best man, your speech will be the last speech of the day, which gives plenty of time for the guests to relax and your nerves to kick in!

• Try to relax and take it easy.

• Try not to look for Dutch courage in the bottom of your wineglass – you'll do your speech more harm than good!

• Keep busy with your other best man duties, organizing the ushers, reading messages, looking after and introducing guests and so on; this will help you to focus, and keep away those pre-speech nerves.

• Listening to the other speeches before yours will help take your mind off your nerves, and laughing will help you relax.

• Have your notes with you, even if you've committed your speech to memory. If your mind goes blank or you feel yourself veering off the point, at least you can refer to them, to get back on track.

• End your speech with a toast – it will give you something to work towards and be a clear signal that your bit is over.

Winning lines

To help spice up your speech, we've put together some original lines that can help flesh out your material – and maybe help you get a laugh or two!

We've divided them up into useful chunks, so it's easy to find what you're after. Obviously, they are just suggestions, but by using your imagination you should be able to adapt them to your own speech perfectly.

Here you'll find lines to help you kick off your speech, and others you can adapt to get a laugh just as you're introducing a new story, or winding one up. And if you're not good at the sentimental stuff, we've got lines to put a tear in your audience's eye.

A common mistake best men make is to say nothing at all about the bride in their speech. So we've included a selection of lines you can use to say something nice – or acceptably naughty – about the bride, too.

Lines to kick off with...

'For the second time today, I rise nervously from a warm seat with a piece of paper in my hand...'

'Fornication, fornication... for-an-occasion such as this, it's an honour to stand here as the best man for the marriage of my dear friends Tom and Mary...'

'For those of you who bet on me giving a speech under three minutes in the sweepstake, you could be in the money. Thanks and goodnight.'

'I asked my Dad for some advice about making this speech today and he said: don't mention politics, sex or religion. Sadly, I never tend to take his advice. So, Tony Blair walks into the confessional wearing stockings and suspenders, and the priest says...'

'When David asked me to be his best man it came as quite a shock. I'd only known him a year. But then I guess you get close very quickly when you're sharing a cell...'

Lines to get a laugh...

'I'm sure you'll all agree that the ushers look very smart in their outfits today. And I think they did a really fantastic job, er… ushing people to their seats. Not an easy job with this kind of crowd, I can tell you. Funny, though, the only other time I've seen them all together wearing suits is in court. Don't forget to call your parole officers tonight, fellas.'

'I've been privileged to know these two as a couple for over five years now. And in all that time I don't think I've once heard them have a row or say a cross word to each other. Rebecca has had nothing but sweet, kind things to say about Richard, and vice versa. They're affectionate towards each other, and kind and considerate towards their friends and family. I give the marriage six months…'

'First of all, I'd like to say what an absolutely fantastic spread that was. A wonderfully generous meal, and so much of it. In fact, I think I might have overeaten. [Looks across the room to someone seated near the back] Tony, could you undo my belt, please? You're nearer…'

'Well done to Tina for catching the bouquet at the church. It looked like it meant a lot to you. And well done for finding a pair of wicket-keeping gloves that match your hat, too…'

'I thought the flowers looked beautiful in the church today. The way the carnations perfectly complemented the pink in the bridesmaids' dresses was a wonderful touch. And to all the girls out there, I am single, by the way, and a really sensitive guy…'

'I'm sure that you'd all agree with me that everything has gone fantastically smoothly so far. In fact, I've heard rumours in the Smith household that they're going to be starting their own wedding planning service with global headquarters at 65 Acacia Avenue…'

'I'd like to thank Emma for being the best thing that's ever happened to Richard. She's looked after him, kept him smiling, been there for him through thick and thin, taught him a few manners, improved his dress sense enormously and, most importantly, taken him off our hands at last.'

'Look at the bride and groom, ladies and gentlemen. Don't they make a lovely couple? They complement each other perfectly. They go together like bacon and eggs, like Yin and Yang, like Morecambe and Wise… like love and marriage, in fact.'

'Ladies and gentlemen, don't you think everything looks fantastic today? I'm talking particularly, of course, about the fabulous marquee in the garden. It certainly does your heart good to see such a big erection at a wedding.'

'I've known Sarah and Jim for a long time and I'm sure everyone will agree with me when I say that they are experts in the art of conversation. In fact, I was really pleased when they asked me to make this speech as it's possibly my first and last chance to get up and talk to them for ten minutes without fear of interruption.'

'I'd like to thank the groom for toasting the bridesmaids – they look great. It's a shame that the same can't be said of the ones at the wedding I went to a few weeks ago. True, both bride and groom are keen bikers, but surely putting everyone in matching leather was going a bit too far...'

'Poor old Steve's mild dyslexia put a spanner in the works when it came to the proposal. He sent Jenny a note asking: "Will you be my waif?" Luckily she took the whole thing in the right spirit and wrote back saying: "Of course I will, you silly banker"...'

'They say that when you start thinking about getting married, you should, in fact, be looking for three different types of woman. The first is a woman who can give you children and raise a family. The second is a woman who can cook majestically. And the third is someone who is exceptionally romantic and a bit of a firebrand in the bedroom. Of course, it's difficult to find all three of these qualities in one woman. If you do, they say, you should marry her straight away. If you don't, they say, you should make sure that the three of them never, ever meet!'

'I think it's great that the happy couple have managed to bridge the age gap between them. Clare is, of course, several years younger than Tom. Actually, it could have been a problem early on in their relationship when Tom took Clare to see Spandau Ballet. She had never heard of them and turned up outside the Shepherd's Bush Empire in a full-length evening gown and her best pearls, expecting a night watching *The Nutcracker*, instead of spending the evening with a bunch of balding New Romantics…'

'I've got a couple of faxes to read out here. The first is from a Suzy Wong in Thailand. It reads: "Hey, Big Boy. How come you no write no more? How come you no send money no more? When you come to Bangkok again? The kids all miss you very much. Suzie."'

'I've kept some of the text messages that Dan sent me during his courtship with Louise. I've got them here and I thought I'd read out a series of four, the contents of which sum up very neatly their blossoming relationship. The first reads: "Tim, met a cracking bird. She's hot. Keep you posted. Dan." The second reads: "Going great with Louise. Think she could be the one. God she's a babe. Dan." The third reads: "Tonight could be the night with Lou. Bit drunk. Hope it goes okay. D." The final one reads: "Wah-hey-heyyyyyyyyyyyyyyy!!!" [pause] They were all sent to me between the hours of 7pm and 3am on the night of 13 March, 1999.'

'I looked up my stars this morning for the first time in ages, to see what was predicted and how I'd get on today. But, to be honest, I don't really believe in fate or any of that mystical stuff, which is odd for a Libran…'

'I know some of the lads were a bit disappointed that today's wedding is being held on Cup Final day. It was especially disappointing for all of the Manchester United fans who've had to travel here from Scotland, Ireland, Wales, Singapore, Australia and, of course, Devon. I believe one has even had to come from Burnage.'

'I know that the honeymoon destination is shrouded in secrecy. Rich has made sure that Emma doesn't know where he is taking her for their three romantic weeks alone. When he was quizzed about it at the stag do, all he would say was that it wasn't far away, it was hot and steamy and there were plenty of water sports. By the sounds of it, Emma, you could be spending three weeks in your bathroom.'

Lines about the groom...

'Rob is hardly what you might call a romantic. I asked him what his first meeting with Teri was like. He said it was like something out of *Brief Encounter*. I had visions of Trevor Howard and Celia Johnson, but Rob told me he bumped into her at the underwear counter in Marks and Spencer's.'

'I remember, just after Tony and Annabel got together, that I asked this self-styled New Man what his perfect night in is, now that he's met the girl of his dreams. Without hesitation he said: "Good bottle of white wine, *Sleepless in Seattle*, an aromatherapy bath and then an early night." I was taken aback. Then he added: "And I'd probably invite Annabel along too."'

'It's fair to say that Dan likes to have a drink once in a while. And he doesn't mind where. In fact, his local is so rough even the arms on the chairs have tattoos. We were playing the trivia machine the other day and the first question was: "What are you looking at, you porky-faced loser?"'

'Josh and I were in the Cub Scouts together. He was my sixer and I was his seconder and together we ran one of the tightest units in the history of Baden-Powell's movement. I hope you still remember some of the things we were taught all those years ago, mate. With your wedding night coming up, I hope you've given your woggle a polish and that you've come prepared...'

'Just one more email for Justin that I quickly picked up from your inbox this morning. I haven't had a chance to read it yet. It goes: "Dear Justin, I'm sorry to hear that the cream does not appear to be working. Are you sure you're rubbing it in hard enough? Nothing will happen unless you can generate plenty of heat with the friction. If you still have no luck, come and see me. Yours faithfully, George Patterson, French polishers and furniture restorers." Oh, I see... I thought it was something to do with... Thank God for that.'

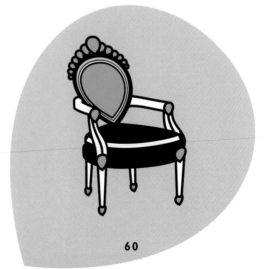

'To end on a slightly more serious note. For those of you who don't know, Rob has grade one tap dancing (with distinction) and has offered to give us all a demonstration of his tap skills in the bar afterwards. I thank you!'

'We all know Tony likes a drink… or six. He told me, though, that he was going to cut down, now that he and Susie have got together permanently. In fact, on the morning after the stag do, I caught Tony mumbling: "I'm never touching another drop, EVER again," while slumped over the lav.'

'Knowing Rob's Dad as well as I do, I knew he'd be a great person to go to for some advice about the speech. I thought he would have some funny anecdotes about Rob to tell me, and that he could give me some general pointers about style and tone. So I went to ask for his advice and all he said to me was: "Make the speech just like Rob." I looked at him quizzically and he added: "Short, punchy and simple."'

'I think it's fair to say that Pete wasn't the best-looking baby on his entry into the world. For one thing, he was the only infant in the whole of Cardiff who was fed by catapult…'

'James was the tallest lad in his primary school. He was 17 years old by the time he passed the entrance exam to secondary school…'

'Dave wasn't the brightest lad at school. I remember the teacher asked him to look up "camouflage" in the dictionary. He said he couldn't find it. So the teacher asked him to look up "laziness" but he said he couldn't be bothered…'

'Terry has never been much of a cook. He used to think poached eggs were stolen property. The last time he made a boil-in-the-bag curry he ruined a perfectly good hold-all.'

'Never one for social etiquette, Neil is the only man I know who orders steak tartare… WELL DONE! He was in a restaurant the other day and sent his crème brûlée back because it was burnt. As he said to me only the other week, he's putting the "K" back into culture.'

'I wouldn't say that Richard is obsessed with fast cars, but he did tell me that he'd bought a brand new pair of driving gloves for the honeymoon. I hadn't realized myself that Rich was so keen on cars until I started talking to him about Annette. Everything he said about her had a driving theme. He said she was racy, made his engine rev… and drove him round the bend.'

'I wouldn't say that Mike is obsessed with playing golf, but he did confide in me that he'd bought a new "Big Bertha" for the honeymoon. For those of you not in the know, that's a rather expensive golf club…'

'I wouldn't say that Ben is obsessed with cricket, but he did tell me that he was taking his pads and helmet on the honeymoon to the West Indies. Now, that might sound a little risqué but, believe me, Ben is taking them just in case he gets a game. In all seriousness, though, Ben said to me the other day that he can't imagine ever making a better catch than the lovely Sally, even if he lived to play cricket until he was 100.'

'I wouldn't say that Chris is obsessed with fishing, but he did tell me that he'd bought a new tackle box for the honeymoon. But when I spoke to him about marrying Linda, he said to me in all his years of fishing – and in all the years to come – he doesn't think he's going to make as good a catch as landing Linda. She really is an angelfish, don't you agree?'

'I wouldn't say that Mike is obsessed with rugby, but he did tell me that he'd bought a new scrum cap for the honeymoon… just in case there's a game on in Sardinia, where they're staying.'

'When Tim and I were playing golf a few months ago, he turned to me on the fifth tee and said solemnly: "Jamie, you're my best man. I need some advice for the honeymoon." Now by this point I had read every book under the sun about the best man's duties. But in none of them was there the slightest mention of having to give the groom advice about the honeymoon. Without being able to look him in the eye, all I could say was: "Listen, mate. I think the best thing to do is keep it simple and make sure you have plenty of rest when you can." He turned to me and said: "Actually I was going to ask you whether you think we should go on safari or have a beach holiday."'

Lines that are sentimental...

'Before I get onto my detailed and, at times, unnecessarily cruel character assassination of my oldest and best friend, I just wanted to say a couple of serious things. First, Rob, I'd like to say that being asked to be your best man is one of the great honours in my life. Thank you. Second, you're the best best friend any guy could ask for. Third, I sincerely hope that the two of you have the most wonderful, happy and long life together and I look forward to sharing with you its highs and lows. Cheers!'

'Before I start my embarrassing revelations about the side of Tom only his best mates get to see, I'd like to take a moment and raise a glass to the bride. Emma is a very special girl and, I think, looks absolutely gorgeous today. To the bride!'

'It's a real shame about the weather. I had such high hopes that it was going to be a fine, sunny day today. I'm sure, though, that the happy couple wouldn't have noticed if it was snowing this afternoon. The two of them couldn't take their eyes off each other. It does your heart good to see...'

'Every man hopes to find the perfect woman. In fact, a lot of us spend most of our youth looking for her. Along the way there may be a little bit of heartbreak. But usually there is a lot of fun, too. I know that Andy has had his fair share of heartache and more than his fair share of fun. But now that he's with Suzanne, his search is over. He's found the woman of his dreams. He's the luckiest man alive and I couldn't be happier for him.'

'These two have been almost inseparable since the day they met. All of us who were there the day that they got together realized almost at once that something special had happened. And it certainly came as no surprise to me that these two wonderful people have eventually got married. It was a great surprise, and honour, to be asked to be best man, and for that I thank you Tony. It's a day I will remember for a long time to come.'

'I'm coming to the end of my official duties as best man, which on the one hand is a massive relief, but on the other hand is a real disappointment, because I really don't think that I could ever feel quite as proud as I have done today, and feel so utterly terrified at the same time. However, I thank you both for allowing me to play a part in such a wonderful day.'

'Oscar Wilde once remarked: "All generalizations are dangerous, including this one." With that in mind, I'll refrain from saying that all brides look beautiful on their wedding day and stick to the specific, where I feel I'm on safer ground: Teresa must be the most beautiful bride ever. To the bride!'

'I know it's customary for the best man's speech to be ribald, uncompromising and at times downright nasty about the groom. I just wanted, though, to take the opportunity to raise a glass for absent friends. There are certain people no longer with us who, I know, would want me to raise a glass on their behalf and wish the happy couple a long, prosperous and, above all, happy life together. [add names here if appropriate] To absent friends.'

Lines about the bride...

'We all know that Jeff enjoys a round of golf. Some might argue he plays a little too often. But I've got to say that in all the rounds I've ever played with him, I've never seen him score a more perfect birdie than the one sitting next to him today...'

'It is all the fashion these days for the bride to make a speech on her wedding day. And those of you who know Sally as well as I do will know that she was never going to pass up an opportunity to speak to such a large group of people without interruption. So, without further delay, making her debut performance as the new Mrs Dave Barham, I give you: the one and only Sally!'

'We all know that Jeff likes to play rugby. In fact, he and I have played many times together. A word of warning, Kerry: he likes to go over the top in rucks and tends to shove before the ball's in...'

'I think everyone will agree that the bride looks absolutely stunning today. And I'm not just saying that to avoid getting a clip round the ear from her new husband...'

'In these modern times, it's very much the fashion for the bride to say a few words at the wedding. I asked Susan's father, Roger, whether he thought she might want to say a few words. He looked at me for a moment and said: "I hope not. I've only hired the room for Saturday night."'

'When he first started raving about his new girlfriend, I asked Ian to describe Debbie to me as if she were a car. He said: "She's like a Ferrari. She's got great lines, she's fast, she turns heads, and I can only afford to take her out every now and again..."'

'When he first started raving about her, I asked Tim to describe Emma to me as if she were a cocktail. He thought about this long and hard, and said that she was like a Tequila Sunrise: tall, long, refreshing and enjoyed best with plenty of crushed ice.'

'The first time Gary started talking about Tina, I asked him: "If she were a football team, which team would she be?" After some careful deliberation, he turned to me and said: "She's like Chelsea: glamorous, creative and full of continental sophistication…'

The first time that Neil started talking about Shirley, he described her as a leather sofa. Slightly confused and taken aback, I asked him to explain. "Well," he said, "she's expensive, luxurious, looks fantastic and I love lying for hours in her warm embrace…"'

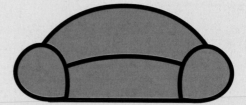

'Karen asked me the other day about Rob's past and, as a good friend of both of them, I thought I ought to fill in any gaps where I could. Obviously, though, out of loyalty to Rob I had to leave out anything that might incriminate him. It was a very short conversation...'

'And now to the bride. "Slovenly", "lazy", "selfish", "pig-headed", "rude", "dirty". These are all words she's used to describe Tim, and with good reason. Frankly, it's a wonder they're together.'

'I'm sure that every man here who knows Katy as well as I do would like to take this opportunity to say that she has never looked as beautiful as she does today. And that's because everyone who knows her as well as I do is also aware that if they don't say that, she'll make sure that they can't ride a bicycle ever again.'

'When Teresa first met Guy, there wasn't what you'd call an instant attraction between them. In fact, I asked Teresa to describe Guy in five words. What were the words she used? Sadly, the only one I can repeat is "and".'

'They say that to find your prince, you have to kiss one or two frogs. Helen, however, has decided to settle for a frog. She always did like wildlife programmes.'

'It was quite some time before I was introduced to Martin's new bride, after they met in Paris where he was working. In one of our telephone conversations, I asked Martin to describe Anne-Marie to me. I imagined his response would be full of elegant language, describing his new French amour in romantic, almost poetic terms. He was hesitant to say anything but after some cajoling he said: "Once you discover her, nothing else will do."'

Lines about the stag do...

'On the subject of the stag do, I'd like to make one comment. Whatever rumours are flying about, Dan did not misbehave. He had a couple of beers with the lads, then went to bed while the single lads went clubbing until seven in the morning. [Turning to the groom] Sorry, mate but they're NEVER going to buy that load of old rubbish.'

'I'd like to take a moment to thank the ushers for their support in organizing the seating in the church, collecting the buttonholes and helping me cut Dan free from being handcuffed to a lamppost on his stag do. I could have sworn I'd brought the keys with me. But thanks for your help anyway, lads.'

Lines about preparing the speech...

'Being best man has made me think long and hard about the commitment of marriage. When I asked my father for his opinion of marriage, he said it was like a playing a long game of chess. "You mean it's easy to learn the rules?" I guessed. "But it takes a lifetime to learn how to play the game successfully." "Not really," he said. "It's more a case of your Mum shouting 'Cheque, mate' every time she sees something she wants…"'

'There's an old adage that goes: "Fail to prepare, prepare to fail." So, with that in mind, I've been fastidious in preparing my speech. It has been meticulously researched, winkling out anecdotes from all the various members of both families about the happy couple. It was neatly typed up and put into my jacket pocket ready for today. Sadly, there is a slightly less well-known but equally useful adage that goes: "Don't leave the jacket with your speech in on the back of a chair in Heston service station on the way up to Tom and Barbara's wedding…"'

'When I was preparing for making this speech today, I thought I should ask a few of my friends who've been best men before for some advice. A friend of ours, Toby, was very forthcoming and said that I should just enjoy it. But he did say that it was the most frightening thing he'd ever experienced in his life, or that he was ever likely to. Bearing in mind he was talking to me from his tank in Basra at the time, I wasn't overly relaxed about what he had said.'

'Once I accepted the role of best man, I started thinking about married life. Being a bachelor, of course, I can only imagine what it must be like. Curious, I asked my dad for an insight into what makes a good marriage. After thinking long and hard, he turned to me and said: "Marriage is like playing a team sport. If everyone doesn't put maximum effort in, then the team will struggle." I was touched and I wanted to talk more. But dad had the ironing to do before vacuuming upstairs, making dinner and picking mum up from the golf club.'

Lines to say thank you to people...

'Now it's my duty to thank the bridesmaids for all their hard work today. I know that Sam and Kerry also organized the hen party. By all accounts you had a great time in Blackpool, especially when a "fireman" called Nick mysteriously appeared in the pub. Something about a magic hose, apparently. Is that right, girls? Sam, you've turned as red as a fire engine.'

'I think you'll agree with me when I say that the reception so far has been absolutely tremendous. It's been a triumph of organization, with absolutely no detail overlooked. Mary, the mother of the bride, told me just before I sat down at the top table that she'd even hired a stand-in best man, just in case my speech got a bit blue and I accidentally stabbed myself in the thigh with her fork...'

'I think a big thank you has to go to Kate, the mother of the bride, for all her intricate planning and attention to detail for the reception. Although I must pull you up on one point Kate. Someone seems to have written a message under my name on my place setting. It reads: "Muck this up, embarrass my family, or tell dirty jokes and you'll never be able to ride a bicycle again. K." I can't imagine how that happened.'

'I'd like to thank the groom for his extremely flattering words about the very beautiful bridesmaids. They certainly all look great today. It might seem strange to those who don't know him as well as I do that Paul is spending his wedding day complimenting other women so fulsomely... but then they don't know Paul as well as I do!'

Sample speeches

To inspire you to create a winning format for your speech, we've put together a selection of full-length sample speeches for you to choose from. Each one has a distinctive format that you can easily adapt to mould your unique material into a cohesive shape.

No matter how well you research your anecdotes, and no matter how funny your stories and jokes, giving your material a recognizable framework will increase the impact of your material enormously. By simply replacing the anecdotes and characters in our sample speeches with your own material, you will quickly see how well each format could work for you.

Sometimes a groom, unable to decide between two lads he's very close to, may opt for two best men. But no matter how good they are, two best man speeches, one after the other, can begin to drag. So we've included a sample speech for a wedding in which two best men speak together. This is still relatively unusual and can make for a memorable speech with a difference.

Sample speech: 'Sticking with tradition'

'Ladies and gentlemen, Jean and Charles [bride's parents], Rodney and Rowena [groom's parents], Mr and Mrs Tate [the newlyweds, pause for a cheer here]…

'It is with great pleasure that I respond to Julian's [the groom's] kind toast on behalf of the bridesmaids. Even though he is too vain to be wearing his bottle-top National Health glasses today, I can confirm, Julian, that the bridesmaids do look as lovely as you just said, even though you were raising your glass to the waitress at the time.

'My other duty today is to regale you with stories of Julian's wicked past. I have to admit this has been tough to prepare for: not due to any shortage of stories but because most of them are too – how can I put this? – colourful to be retold in such refined company. Not counting you, of course, though Dave [to one of the ushers].

'So in the end I thought: where better to begin than on that other auspicious date, thirty-odd (and his life has been odd) years ago, when Julian was born? In 1969, the year of Julian's birth, Neil Armstrong took his first tentative steps on the moon, as Julian took his own first baby steps. His mother tells me Julian also made his own "giant leap for mankind" but, unfortunately, Julian's was off the big slide in the park and resulted in a lovely little scar that I'm sure Helen will be seeing later…

'Also in the year of his birth, the 50p piece was introduced into British currency, as Julian was making his own first little "pees"! It was also the year *Sesame Street* first hit our TV screens, and I'm told that Big Bird was a huge favourite of Julian's. That same year saw the publication of the first issue of *Penthouse* magazine and, er… I'm told that big birds have also been a huge favourite of Julian's.

'But enough of his childhood. I cannot remember exactly when I first met Julian. It could have been at a college lecture. It could have been on the golf course. It could have been in Chasers, our local nightclub. What I do remember clearly is that Julian was slurring his words and falling about the place. So chances are it was in a lecture.

'Julian is a fantastically generous and loyal friend. He's more than happy to come and collect you from your house and drive you to the golf course for a round at any time. He is also happy to coach you in your game with "encouraging" remarks at the very moment you are about to tee off.

'Julian is also a very trusting person. I remember one day when we went en masse to Leeds to visit an old mate for a party. Julian got lost on the way back from the pub and couldn't find where we were staying. Luckily, as he stumbled about the city centre, he bumped into a charming gang of lads who claimed they knew where he was staying and offered to escort him there.

'Arriving back at the student flat, Julian was so overwhelmed by how kind the locals had been, he offered to make them breakfast. A full English and several cups of tea later they left and Julian woke up his hungover mates to say how taken he'd been with his new friends. Taken, it later emerged, was indeed the word for it… his wallet, car keys, watch and mobile phone!

'Still, with Helen to look after him, Julian should be able to avoid such crises in future. I speak on behalf of all his mates, and with total sincerity, when I say that we still can't believe that anyone that lovely has agreed to take him on.

'Perhaps Helen should take some advice from that other paragon of great loveliness, Joanne Woodward, who has said of her own long marriage to Hollywood sex symbol Paul Newman: "Sexiness wears thin after a while and beauty fades, but to be married to a man who makes you laugh every day, ah, now that's a real treat." Helen, as you can see, he's no Paul Newman. But, just looking at him (or his scar), I think we can be sure that he will give you a laugh every day.

'And so ladies and gentlemen, I ask you to raise your glasses to a long, laughter-filled life together for the lovely couple – to Helen and Julian!'

Sample speech: 'Reworking the reading'

'Jeff and Kerry [gesturing to the bride and groom] have finally tied the knot. Congratulations. You both look fantastically happy today, and I'm sure that you're going to have a wonderful life together. How do I know that? Because I know that you love each other, and that's what really counts in a marriage. For, in the words of a famous passage from Corinthians, "If I have no love, I have nothing."'

'I'm sure you all know that reading. So I thought I'd see how Jeff, in particular, compared to the romantic sentiments in the passage. Remember how it begins?

"I may be able to speak the languages of men and even of angels, but if I have no love, my speech is no more than a noisy gong or a clanging bell."

'Well, I don't know if Jeff started off by speaking the language of men or angels on his stag night, but after his fourth Tequila body-slammer he definitely needed an interpreter. But we all got the gist of what he was saying: he loved EVERYONE that night. And he was feeling no pain at that stage of the evening. As for clanging bells, the only one Jeff heard was after he'd set off the fire alarm in the hotel.

'The reading continues:
"I may have the gift of inspired preaching; I may have all knowledge and understand all secrets; I may have all the faith needed to move mountains – but if I have no love, I am nothing."

'Well, Jeff sure thinks he's got all knowledge and I know that he's got plenty of shady secrets, that's for certain. And we all know that he LOVES to talk, especially when he's preaching the virtues of his beloved Tottenham, spreading his expert knowledge of the dance moves in *Staying Alive*, and moving more than mountains after a session at the pub and a lobster vindaloo from the Taj Mahal.

"I may give away everything I have, and even give up my body to be burnt – but if I have no love, this does me no good."

'Jeff is not likely to give away everything he has. For instance, on the stag do he was very particular about keeping his trousers on, I seem to remember, after some of the lads decided they wanted them as a trophy. It was quite a fist-fight, I can tell you. And in the end, his trousers were indeed "given up to be burnt".

"Love is patient and kind; it is not jealous or conceited or proud; love is not ill-mannered or selfish or irritable; love does not keep a record of wrongs; love is not happy with evil, but is happy with the truth."

'The truth. Mmm… we're back to the stag again. I can't really tell anyone the truth about what happened on the stag. Just as we were leaving for Blackpool, Jeff turned to me and said: "What goes on tour, stays on tour. Right, Tim?" I thought to myself: "That sounds like a good call." Anyone who went on the stag, I am sure, will agree this wasn't just a "good" call but an absolutely essential one. And don't forget, everyone: Blackpool magistrates, 11 o'clock Monday. [Looking over to one of the ushers] Neil, you're bringing the donkey, right?

"Love never gives up; and its faith, hope, and patience never fail."

'I think patience is a virtue that Jeff must have in spades. It took him five years to ask Kerry to marry him for a start. How he could wait that long to marry such a wonderful girl is anyone's guess.

"Love is eternal. There are inspired messages, but they are temporary; there are gifts of speaking in strange tongues but they will cease. There is knowledge, but it will pass."

'Speaking of passes, Jeff tells a very romantic story about how he first made a pass at Kerry. Apparently, she was standing in the pub and he handed her a pint and said: "Hold this while I go for a slash, will you?" Such a charmer.

"For our gifts of knowledge and inspired messages are only partial; but when what is perfect comes, then what is partial will disappear."

'I remember when Jeff first described Kerry to me he used the word "perfect". "I tried my usual chat-up line about holding my pint," he recalled, "and when I came back she was perfectly polite when she told me to 'bog off'. How little things have changed. Nearly there now:

"When I was a child, my speech, my feelings, and thinking were those of a child; now that I am a man, I have no more use for childish ways."

'Jeff's always been a bit of a kid at heart. Funnily enough, he was the biggest kid in our class. I remember seeing him for the first time and thinking he was a giant. Then someone told me he'd had to repeat his first year of primary school six times. He was actually 24 when he finally left school.

"What we see now is like a dim image in a mirror; then we shall see face to face. What I know now is only partial; then it will be complete – as complete as God's knowledge of me. Meanwhile these three remain; faith, hope, and love; and the greatest of these is love."

'That's enough from me. Except to say: here's to Jeff and Kerry and THEIR great love. Cheers!'

Sample speech: 'The Two Ronnies'

[This speech can be used when there are two best men. Top tip: don't try and rehearse this too much and make sure that you read it from cards. Trying to learn it verbatim and perform without prompts seldom works as well.]

Best man 1 [BM1]: 'Good evening. Before we get on with the formal parts of the speech, Tim [BM2] and I would just like to read out some headlines.'

BM2: [In a newsreader's voice] 'Good evening and here is the news… from Dave's [the groom] past…'

BM1: '19 February, 1975: A Peterborough couple gave birth today to their son David Algernon Smith, who weighed in at a rather skinny 6lb 11oz. The couple, Peter and Lorraine, were said to be delighted with the newest edition to their family, although Mr Smith was overheard as saying: "I thought you said it was going to be a girl, mother.

'When asked about the baby's diminutive size, Mrs Smith said: "I'm sure he'll put on weight quickly." How right Mrs Smith was then and has been ever since...'

BM2: '26 May, 1989: A young Peterborough boy, David Smith, was thrown out of the Scouts today, after an internal inquiry, led by Bagheera and Akela, found the young rascal guilty of stealing a bottle of wine from a local fête. Smith was unavailable for comment, having been sent to his room without any tea and a smack across the back of his legs.

'The boy's parents were said to be upset and dismayed, according to a close family source.'

BM1: '28 September, 1993: Liverpool University welcomed a highly acclaimed schoolboy academic through its doors, today. David Smith, fresh from his triumphant two Cs and a D at A' level, took his seat in the geography department. He is said to be eager to make the most of his opportunity and wants to be a model student in the tertiary education system.

'"This is a great chance for me to change the way geography is perceived around the world," said Smith on the steps of the Red Lion. "I'm sick of it being ridiculed as a dossers' subject, full of rejects and wannabe town planners," enthused the uncharacteristically frank youngster, known as Smudge by his small circle of friends and fellow layabouts. "I aim to give my degree my best shot and will settle for nothing less than a First."'

BM2: '7 July, 1994: David 'Smudge' Smith was un-cordially invited to "leave the university and never darken the geography department's door again" by leading town planning lecturer 'Pongo' Watson.

'Professor Watson cited several reasons for the dismissal of Smith, concluding that: "The main reason he has been asked to leave is because unlike most students – who usually have poor attendance records – Mr Smith has no attendance record at all."'

'When given the news in bed, at three o'clock this afternoon, a tight-lipped Smith stated: "I'm off to the Union to get pissed."'

BM1: '9 October 1996: Dave 'Hound Dog' (formerly 'Smudge') Smith was spotted talking to a mystery blonde in Shakers nightclub this evening. Having downed several vodkas, three pints of cider and a quantity of Dubonnet, the normally reserved Smith is said to have tackled the stunner – later identified as Kerry Watson, 26, from Plaistow – as she danced with friends.

'He later claimed in court that he wasn't, in fact, trying to 'tackle' her but had lost his footing while crossing the dance floor, stumbled and reached out for the nearest thing available – Ms Watson's chest. After an exchange of verbal machine-gun fire, the two were seen leaving together.'

BM2: '26 December, 1998: In a series of telephone calls today, David Smith – good friend to us all, top bloke and a very lucky man – told of how he had asked Kerry Watson to marry him and she had said "yes".

'"We're going to be so happy together," Smith was heard to say. "And I wasn't even drunk when I asked her." Ms Watson was unavailable for comment. Most unusual.

BM1: 'And that was the news. So it's goodnight from me…'

BM2: 'And goodnight from him.'

Sample speech: 'The appraisal'

'Ladies and gentlemen, it really is an honour to be standing in front of you today as best man to someone as special as Gary [the groom]. I must say that when he asked me, I was totally taken aback. But now I'm standing here I feel nothing but pride. Thanks for such an honour, mate.

'Okay, that was the nice, sincere part of the speech. Now it's time to get down to the nitty-gritty of embarrassing the very man who showed such faith, and yet such poor judgment, in choosing me.

'I thought long and hard about how to theme this speech, and then it suddenly dawned on me that I could use the skills I've picked up as a manager at work. I thought I'd write Katy [the bride] an appraisal of Gary.

'So, first things first: punctuality. Well, Katy, you must have known Gary long enough by now to know that he is not the world's greatest timekeeper. In fact, he's not the world's best when it comes to dates either. Only last week he told me how much he was looking forward to the wedding – on 7 July! Luckily I corrected him and here we are on the 8th… just! We were running late for most of the stag do, too, when Gary managed to miss the train to his own party. So Katy, you have been warned.

'Next we move on to: management skills. As we all know, one of the prerequisites of being a good manager is the art of diplomacy. And I think it's fair to say that Gary is not a man overly blessed with skills in this particular area. I remember we were sitting in French class when we were about 15 and we had a new teacher, Miss Simpson. She had just introduced herself and we were asking her some questions before class began when Gary piped up and asked her when her baby was due. Of course, there was no baby. Poor old, plump Miss Simpson went bright red and the rest of the class fell about. You did rather poorly in your 'O' level French, as I recall, Gary…

'Next on the agenda, Katy, has to be: career prospects. Now Gary is, as I'm sure we'll all agree, very competent at his job. In fact, he has moved steadily through the ranks and is doing very nicely, thanks. But I must say that things could have been so different. I'm told that during his student days, his part time career at a large drinks company [alter as appropriate] was marred by his performance at the first Christmas party he attended all those years ago. Let's look at the ingredients of the disaster, shall we? There was Mr Hobbs [the groom], women and there was a free bar. Needless to say, Mr Hobbs helped himself to the bar, got rather drunk and rather loud and managed to finish the evening off by falling asleep on a desk, with his trousers neatly folded on the back of the chair. Sadly, it wasn't his desk – or chair – but his boss's. Oh, dear…

'Now what about: teamwork? Gary has always been a great team player. He's run the line for pretty much every football team he's tried to play in. He's washed the kit for several rugby clubs he's tried to join, and he makes a cracking tea when the lads play Sunday afternoon cricket. But seriously, though, Gary thrives in a team environment. He's unselfish and supportive when things are going badly, and that's what makes him such a great bloke. He can't play sport for toffee, mind you, but he's a great mascot…

'And finally, Katy, we move on to: extra-curricular activities. There's no point in denying that Gary thought of himself as a bit of a ladies' man at college. It turned out, however, that he was only chatting up different girls all the time because he couldn't find one that was interested. His favourite chat-up line at the time was: "We don't need to take our clothes off to have a good time. Let's just drink some cherry wine." I rest my case.

'So, Katy, that's my appraisal of Gary. It's too late to back out now. You'll just have to make a fist of it and see what happens. But what I do know is that he loves you very much and that you're going to have a great life together. To the happy couple!'

Sample speech: 'Reality TV interview'

'Ladies, gentlemen, boys, girls… and Rob it gives me great pleasure to be standing here today. In fact, I feel totally honoured to have the responsibility of ritually humiliating my best friend in front of those he loves.

'Added to that, I can't tell you how nice it is to be able to talk with Rob in the room, safe in the knowledge that he can't interrupt me. In the 15 years I've known him, this must be the first time that has ever happened. I think I should take complete advantage of the situation, don't you?

'I was thinking of how I could structure this speech. Then it suddenly occured to me how much Rob loves reality TV shows like *Big Brother* and *I'm a Has-been, Vote to Keep Me in this Hell-hole* – or whatever it's called. So, I thought it might be fun to imagine what sort of things Rob would put on an application form for one of these shows [picks up clipboard]. Now let me see…'

'Age: 20.

'Now, no matter what Rob does, he always maintains that he still feels like a 20-year-old. Sadly, the thinning hair and the paunch give him away.

'Sex: Yes, please. I don't think I need add to that.

'Skills: Leadership, organization and bronze medal life-saving.

'I think Rob has had several important leadership roles in his life so far. He was to all intents and purposes the leader of our gang when we were kids. Sadly, under his leadership we got into quite a bit of trouble. In fact, Rob was the youngest lad in our school to have a criminal record. *Agadoo*, by Black Lace, I believe it was.

'Organization is not really his strong point either. I remember at college he was president of the Real Ale Society and had the job of organizing the annual event of the Real Ale Society Oompah Band Beer Festival. The hall was booked, the posters put up, the fliers handed out. The band turned up on time and a few punters even paid to get in. Unfortunately, the chairman – our Rob – had forgotten to bring the Real Ale Soc cheque book, so when the beer delivery arrived we couldn't pay for it. Rob really couldn't organize a piss-up in a brewery.

'And as for the bronze medal life-saving badge, Rob is very proud of it. So proud, in fact, that he appeared on holiday once with it sewn on his swimming trunks. Shame he was 23 at the time.

'Hobbies and interests: windsurfing, chess, socializing and reading.

'Now I know that Rob still thinks of himself as a bit of a blade when it comes to windsurfing, despite not having donned his wetsuit for several years... well, he wore it on the stag weekend but that's a different matter. He certainly knows the rules of chess, but the last time I said "Check mate" to him, he replied: "I don't owe you any money, do I?" A more accurate description of his idea of socializing would be: going to the pub – any pub. And the only reading he does these days is the menu at the Taj Mahal, or the *Racing Post*.

'Sum up in 50 words why you want to appear on the show: "I think I'd be a great contestant because I'm funny, intelligent, tolerant, a great leader, a fantastic team player and good with my hands."

'Mmm... where to start? I think I'd probably just add one word to that long list of glowing attributes and that's "modest".

'So there you have it. That's how I think Rob would fill in his application form and that's how I think I would correct it. As for the show that Rob would most suit and do well on? *Big Brother* is out because he couldn't handle life without TV. *Survivor* is a non-starter because of his fear of spiders. (By the way, did you know that Rob is a closet *Take the High Road* fan? Didn't miss one episode in three years of college.)

'Ah! I've got it. It would have to be *Pop Idol*, because Rob's definitely one of the most popular guys I know. And he's one of the most idle. Please be upstanding for the bride and groom. The bride and groom.'

Sample speech: 'The political agenda'

'Given the fact that Tim [the groom] is such an incredibly popular and successful man, it seems doubly amazing to me that he's asked me to be his best man. There must have been dozens of candidates. But then I am his oldest friend. I suppose the first thing I should do is to say thank you. And I suppose the second thing I should do is say sorry. Because while it is an honour to be standing here as your best man, it is also my duty to be really nasty about you, too.

'In fact, the first thing I did when I was asked to make this speech was ask Tim's doctor, who shall remain nameless, what he thought of the groom-to-be. The doctor said that, in his professional opinion, Tim was "clinically lazy, a compulsive liar and mildly neurotic". Shocked, I asked for a second opinion. He said: "Okay then, he's an ugly bugger with smelly feet."

'But enough of that. Let's get on with the speech. I thought, seeing as Tim has shown such an active and ideologically fluid interest in politics over the years, that it would be interesting to imagine what his election manifesto would look like, should he ever run for office. Now I know you should never discuss politics, sex or religion at the dinner table. But seeing as my only alternative is to tell the story about George W. Bush, a one-legged lady-of-the-night and the Reverend Ian Paisley, I think I'm on safer ground with the manifesto.

'What about foreign affairs? Well, Tim is all in favour. I've accompanied him on several trips abroad, all of which have involved attempted diplomatic "liaisons" with various local girls. But none was ever that successful. In fact, there was one time in France when he tried to use a romantic chat-up line. He meant to say to a rather stunning young mademoiselle: "*Vous êtes très belle, je voudrais vous embrasser,*" meaning, "You're very beautiful, I'd like to kiss you." But instead he said: "*Vous êtes très folle, je devrais vous enlacer*", meaning: "You're very mad, I'm going to have to tie you up." Tim with his own version of the *entente cordiale* there...

'Let us turn to education. Tim believes that every person should get the most out of the system. This explains why he spent two years in the third form at school, resat his A' levels twice and started two degrees before gaining a Second in Social Anthropology from Hull University. It has also been brought to my attention that, while at primary school, Tim availed himself of all the activities on offer, including taking part in the school Nativity play. He had a starring role as Third Sheep. Of course, right on cue his fellow sheep went "baa" and he went [pause] "moo".

'How about law and order? Tim has seen the activities of the police force up close, and is no stranger to the workings of the magistrates courts. After a rather merry evening at his local about a year ago, Tim decided to water the plants in someone's garden on the way home. Unfortunately, just as he was sprinkling the geraniums, two of Her Majesty's Constabulary happened upon him and he wound up in the nick for the night.

'Where does Tim stand on economics? Well, he most certainly believes in the free market. He's always coming up with hair-brained, get-rich-quick-schemes. A bit like the time he decided to hold a jumble sale in his front garden without telling his mum and dad. To make things worse, he wasn't just selling his old toys but also the contents of the family's front room. I must say that the brand-new video I picked up for 50p was the best bargain I've ever had. Lovejoy would have been proud!!

'So there you have it: Tim's manifesto. As you can tell, he's a man of strong principles and fine ethics. So long as they disregard his politics, I know that he and Hayley will make a fantastic couple.

'Let me end now on a serious and sincere note by wishing today's lucky couple all the happiness in the world. Please raise your glasses and be upstanding for the bride and groom!'

Sample speech: 'A day in the life of...'

'Without a shadow of a doubt, this is the most nerve-wracking thing I have ever done. But at the same time it is a great honour to have been picked by Ken [the groom] as his best man. When he phoned to let me know, I nearly choked with surprise and I had a huge lump in my throat. That'll teach me to talk on the phone when I'm eating a kebab.

'Anyway, I thought long and hard about what I wanted to say in this speech. Obviously, Karen [the bride] has known Ken for many years. She's seen his career flourish, his hair fall out and his paunch widen.

'However, I realized that it's my duty to let Karen know what Ken was like BEFORE she met him. Obviously, since he met his beloved wife-to-be, Ken has been on his best behaviour. But I can assure that hasn't always been the case.

'Ken and I have been best friends since primary school, so I have been witness to some of Ken's finer moments. I've also, of course, been witness to some of his less than fine moments. And, naturally, it's those moments that I feel I should tell Karen about – in front of just about everyone Ken cares about.

'How best to catalogue such a huge number of embarrassing moments? Well, I thought I would put them together on a CV to support Ken's application for the job of Karen's husband. OK, so he's already landed the job – but just bear with me…

'Let's start with his qualifications, shall we? An impressive ten O' levels, three A' levels and a second class honours degree in Sports Science from Lancaster University. Ken also holds various gymnastics badges, 17 merit badges (including needlework!) from Scouts, and a Winner's Certificate – from our Club 18–30 holiday to Santa Ponsa, Majorca – in the Drink-As-Much-Sangria-As-You-Can-Before-Passing-Out contest, 1993.

'Let us take a look now in more detail at Ken's glittering academic career.

'1981–1983: Busy Bee nursery school. [mimicking the groom's voice] "I spent three years honing my excellent communication skills at this prestigious school, where my love of drama flourished. I appeared in several productions, playing Lead Toadstool, Second Sheep and Mr Frog, before a controversial starring role as Pontius Pilate in the school Nativity play."

'1983–1989: Clifton Manor primary school. "In a distinguished career at Clifton, I became one of the most popular boys in the school. This was because, for several years, I conned my mum into giving me dinner money, when in fact we were given lunch at the school. I used this money to build up a small stock of sweets, comics and pictures of Page 3 models, which formed the basis of a highly successful black market operation run from behind the athletics equipment hut.

'1989–1994: Stoneybrook secondary school. "As well as a successful record in both O' and A' levels at Stoneybrook, I was also the first student to dye my hair orange for mufti day, and the only student to receive a suspension for drinking cider in the language labs. In the sporting arena, I excelled in the area of cross-country, holding the school record for nearly two years. Unfortunately, the title was taken away from me in a rather ignominious fashion, when the games master realized that the time I had recorded was, in fact, close to the world record for 5,000 metres. I had, of course, hidden in a bush for the duration of the race, reappearing, complete with muddy legs and flushed cheeks, only a few minutes later to jog home. My appeal, lodged with the International Athletics Federation in 1992, is pending."

'1995–1999: Lancaster University. "While at college, I was an active member of the student body. I joined the Real Ale society, the Wine Society and the Soul, Funk & Reggae Society, and was a regular attender at all the social events organized by each. I also gained several honours during my time there. I am still the only Sports Science student ever to be reprimanded for poor attendance in lectures, having only managed four in six terms. I held the Yard of Ale record for three terms and am still, to my knowledge, the only student to have run up a four-figure overdraft with three of the five major high street banks.

'19 March, 2000 (the day I met Karen) – present: "I am now enjoying the best time of my life, and continue to be the luckiest man alive since meeting the love of my life."

'Ladies and gentlemen, I give you the groom and his wonderful, beautiful bride.'

Sample speech: 'Emails'

'Distinguished guests, ladies, gentlemen, boys and girls, I stand before you a very proud and a very privileged man. I have been accepted into the prestigious Mill Hill Golf and Country Club, which is an absolute dream come true. I know you'll all join me in celebrating with a quick toast. To me!

'Now let's get on with the best man's speech. I must say it was quite nice of Tony [the groom] to ask me, and if I hadn't been preparing for the Mill Hill interview, I would probably have been more excited than I am right now.

'Seriously, though, it really is a fantastic honour to be standing in front of you as Tony's best man. We've known each other since we were at school, and I think it's fair to say we've been through quite a bit together. That doesn't mean, though, that we've spent all of our time together. We were at different colleges, in different countries, in different jobs. But we've stayed in touch by email over the years.

'So what I thought I'd do is read out some of this electronic correspondence, to give you a flavour of Tony's life over the years. His may not be the easiest of prose styles to read, but what he lacks in finesse he makes up for in... bluntness.

'Here's the first one. Subject line is: "Freshers' week – totally bonkers!" And it continues: "Dear Robereeno, Finally got to De Montfort after the fiasco with my A' levels. How could I have failed Home Economics? Anyway, looking forward to getting stuck into my course. I always preferred Drama, anyway. Just had a mad week drinking myself purple and chasing women. Really digging the college vibe, man. Thinking of joining CND and the Communist Party. How things with you? T"

'Fairly standard stuff. Here's one dated two years into college. Subject line: "Those Commie bastards!" And we read on: "Dear Rob, Just been chucked out of the Communist Party for saying that Mrs Thatcher might have been unfairly represented in the UK press. Nazis, the lot of 'em. Course is crap. Still can't get laid and my grant has run out. Can't wait to get out of this pit. Thinking of a career in the army or the police. Anthony."

'Interesting shift in tone in that one, I thought. Now here's one from a couple of weeks after he first met Chantelle [the bride]. Subject line reads: "She is the ONE!" And it goes: "Mate, Just got back from a wicked party. Met this amazing chick. She had some kind of foreign-sounding name: Chartreuse or something like that. She's absolutely fit as a butcher's dog with…" I'll just skip those couple of lines. Er… anyway: "We talked all night and she was well into me. I had her eating out of the palm of my hand. She could be the ONE, mate. Keep you posted. Ant. PS Things with you okay?"

'Three months later I got this one. Subject line: "I'm actually engaged – can you believe it?" And it goes: "Just a quickie to let you know that Chants and I are getting hitched. Asked her as we watched the sun go down over Table Mountain. Travelling is great. Speak to you when I get back. A."

'Several years on, and one or two temporary separations later, I received this one. Subject line: "Diary date." The message simply says: "R, C and I marriage. Keep 15 Jul free. A. PS U R BM."

'And so, here we are. There have obviously been hundreds more emails between us, but I thought those would just give you a taste of how Tony has matured over the years, and how he's become rather more taciturn. And here's one I sent to him, when he told me I was going to be best man.

"'Tony, I only just got your email today. I've been at the Golf Club quite a bit recently and haven't logged on. I was absolutely delighted to hear that you and Chantelle are finally going to tie the knot. And I'm bursting with pride that you've chosen me to be your best man. It would be an honour."

"'I've always thought I was a lucky man to have such a warm, kind and considerate bloke as you as my best mate. And now, to be your best man, well, that's the cherry on the cake. I know you and Chants will be very happy. You're a very lucky man."

"'All the best, old chum. I look forward to the big day with immense anticipation. Your best bud, always. Rob.
PS Got into Mill Hill a couple of days ago. We'll have to go for a game soon."

'Ladies and gentlemen, I give you the wonderful couple.'

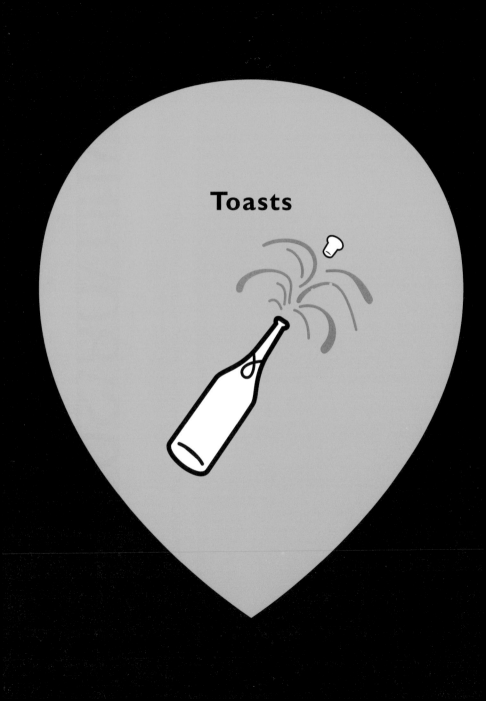

Toasts

As best man it's your duty to end your speech with a toast to the bride and groom. To help you round off your speech with a flourish, choose a toast from this selection and adapt it to fit in smoothly with the rest of your material.

Some couples don't want a series of long speeches at the reception and will ask you to make a simple toast instead. In fact, all wedding speeches are glorified toasts really, so if you're asked to give a toast only, think of it as a mini-speech. As best man, you may end up doing both if, for instance, there's a rehearsal dinner before the wedding, or post-wedding drinks for guests.

Remember that the toast should come at the very end of your speech. It will be an anti-climax and you'll cause confusion if, after everyone has raised their glasses and made the toast, you then carry on speaking!

Give everyone a moment to charge their glasses, be very clear in the exact wording of the toast – 'To the adorable couple!' – join in the toast… then sit down and enjoy the applause. Job done!

Classic best man's toasts

'So I'd like you all to charge your glasses and join me in toasting the new Mr and Mrs Brown. Ladies and gentlemen, I give you the bride and groom.'

'Wishing them all the health, wealth and happiness in the world, I'd like you all to join me in toasting the happy couple. Ladies and gentlemen, the bride and groom.'

'Now it only remains for me to get you all on your feet. And with charged glasses [pause], I'd like you to join me in toasting the new Mr and Mrs Roberts. Ladies and gentlemen, I give you the wonderful bride and groom.'

'And now all I have left to do is to say what a privilege it is to ask you all to charge your glasses and – for those of you who still can! – rise to your feet. Ladies and gentlemen – the bride and groom.'

'Ladies and gentlemen, will you please join me now in toasting two young – well, quite young! – people who have everything, because [looks at couple] you love each other. Ladies and gentlemen, the lucky couple.'

'To finish with some words from the bard: "Love comforteth like sunshine after rain." So, you two, I hope your marriage is full of intermittent drizzle, followed by days of blistering heat. To the bride and groom.'

'To the adorable couple – Mark and Lisa.'

'Jerry – my best friend – some words of advice in the form of a wise old poem. "To keep a marriage brimming with love in the loving cup, when you are wrong, admit it, and when you are right, shut up!" To Jerry and Claire!'

'Here's to the two things that – without doubt – make a great marriage. Here's to a good sense of humour, and selective hearing. Ladies and gentlemen – the bride and groom.'

'Before we toast the happy couple, here's to wives and lovers everywhere – and to them never, ever meeting!'

'If ever there was a competition for the best-suited couple, Posh and Becks needn't bother entering, because I think they're sitting just a few feet away from me. No, not you Ted and Edith, I'm talking about the new Mr and Mrs Grimshaw. Ladies and gentlemen, it gives me immense pleasure to ask you to raise your glasses and toast – the bride and groom!'

'I'd like to end by toasting the bride and groom. But just before I do, I'd like to say some lines from a song to the groom, Richard. The song was written many years ago but the lyrics, I believe, are still meaningful today. [Speak the words, with no tune] "She loves you, yeah, yeah, yeah. She loves you, yeah, yeah, yeah, yeah. And with a love like that, you know you should be glad." 'Ladies and gentlemen, I give you the bride and groom.'

'I asked my dad, joker that he is, what type of toast I should propose at the wedding and he replied: "French". *Bon, sans vous faire attendre un instant de plus, Mesdames et Messieurs, je vous présente... Monsieur et Madame Jones. Les nouveaux mariés! A John et Jude!*'

'Before I offer a toast to Tony and Marie, I'd like to leave you with one thought: You don't marry someone you can live with, you marry someone you can't live without. In this case, these two really have married the right person. To the bride and groom.'

'Just before I ask you to raise your glasses in a toast to the happy couple, I'd like to paraphrase an old adage. It goes: if you've got love in your lives, then that's great because you don't really need anything else. And if you haven't got love, it doesn't really matter what else you've got. To a couple always destined to have each other – Bob and Mary!'

Stand-alone toasts

Toasts like these can be used, where required, in place of longer speeches and/or at a rehearsal dinner...

Formidable team

'Ladies and gentlemen, thanks very much for indulging me for a few moments. As you may be aware, the bride and groom didn't want to have a series of long speeches. I can't tell you how happy I felt when I heard that. I would, however, like to thank the groom for his kind words.

'It's only left to me, then, to toast the bride and groom. But before I do, I'd like to take this opportunity, on behalf of friends and family gathered here today, to wish this fantastic couple all the happiness in the world. Graham and Julie really are smashing people as individuals, and together they make a truly formidable team. The two of them are tighter than the spring that keeps Graham's wallet shut...

'So, without further delay, please be upstanding, raise your glasses and toast the bride and groom – the bride and groom!'

Nature's strongest force

'Unaccustomed as I am to public speaking, it gives me great pleasure to stand before you today – all of Darren and Sarah's nearest and dearest – with the supreme honour of being their best man.

'When Darren asked me to be his best man, he told me categorically that he didn't expect me to make a long speech. He knows how embarrassed and nervous I get talking to myself in the mirror, let alone standing up in front of the most important people in his and Teresa's lives.

'However, now I'm here, I would like to make a couple of observations. The first is that Darren, in all the time that I have known him, has never looked forward to or been more excited about something than he has been about today – even when Wrexham reached the third round of the DAF Trucks Trophy in the 1986/7 season.

'The two of them look dazzling today, especially the way the lights are shining off Darren's bald patch. It looks like he's polished it especially. And he's worn a suit, which I know for a fact he hasn't done since the stag do… or rather, the court appearance soon after it.

'Anyway, without further delay – the bride and groom.'

Final words of wisdom

So you've done all your research, gathered all your anecdotes and written one hell of a speech and/or toast. You've made sure that it contains all of the formal stuff, with a healthy dose of (not too) irreverent stories about the groom.

Maybe there's even the odd sentimental word in there about how honoured you are to have been chosen as best man, or how much the groom means to you as a mate. And, of course, you haven't totally neglected the bride, and you've included some nice words about her, too.

All you need to do now is get up there and give the speech. But before you do, here are some final words of advice to make sure you do the best job possible on the big day.

Practise, practise, practise

'The more I practise,' said golfing legend Gary Player, 'the luckier I get.' Ask Tiger Woods or David Beckham how they became the best in their professions and they'll tell you it's all down to practice. Whatever your levels of confidence and competence at the moment of taking on this important job of the speech, putting time into your preparation will reap serious improvements.

Use your partner, your family or close friends as guinea pigs, running through the whole thing with them at least a couple of times. This will give you a chance to iron out any wrinkles in the text, hone the delivery of your punchlines and change anything that really doesn't work.

Remember whose day it is

You're not the star of the show – the bride and groom are. Remember that, as best man, you're supposed to be playing a supporting role, not taking centre stage. Obviously you want to entertain people, but if you do so at the expense of the bride and groom and their enjoyment of the day, you'll have failed in your duties, however many laughs you get from the crowd.

or many people, having a few drinks when nervous is a way
of relaxing and calming the nerves. As you watch the rest of
the wedding party getting sozzled, why shouldn't you?

Try and resist that temptation at all costs. One glass too
many will only diminish your judgment and you could find
yourself telling that embarrassing, or worse still, offensive
joke without realizing what you're doing. Reward yourself
with a drink – after the speech.

Keep to the script

Ideally you'll have put your speech – if not verbatim, then
in note form – on to prompt cards. Use them to keep
your speech flowing and to make sure that you don't miss
anything important out. But equally important, make sure
you don't start adding things in.

If the speech is going well, your confidence will soar and you
may think that you should spice up a perfectly good, well-
rehearsed speech with additional material. Unless you are a
really experienced performer, stick to what you've practiced.

Don't panic

No one knows what you're going to say in your speech. So if,
for whatever reason, you skip a section, lose your place or
simply dry up, don't worry. Most people won't know that
you've gone wrong. Simply pause, find a place where you can

Speak up, slow down

No matter how good your material is, and no matter how well you've rehearsed your gags, if your audience can't hear you, they're never going to laugh. The most common mistakes a best man can make are to mumble, talk to the floor and/or talk at a million miles an hour – worst, all of these at once! Speak up and slow down, and you'll be fine.

Never heckle hecklers

No one in the room wants to see the best man fail to make a great speech. But, when the nerves are jangling and the adrenaline is pumping, being interrupted by someone in the crowd can seem like the rudest thing you've ever heard in your life. You may be sorely tempted to tell the clever dick to keep their thoughts to themselves. Don't.

If someone heckles you, roll with it. Some people like to join in with the speeches at weddings, and they almost certainly don't mean any harm. More often than not the things people shout out are very funny. Laugh along with them and you'll find it helps you to relax.

And finally...

Think of your speech as a gift to your friends. It's an honour to have been asked, so see your words as a token of your appreciation, as well as your own contribution to the specialness of their day. Above all, enjoy yourself. If you're having a good time, and are speaking with goodwill, you cannot fail to warm your audience, too.

INDEX

Confetti.co.uk is the UK's leading wedding and special occasion website, helping more than 400,000 brides, grooms and guests every month.

Confetti.co.uk is packed full of ideas and advice to help organize every stage of your wedding. At confetti, you can choose from hundreds of beautiful wedding dresses; investigate our list of more than 3,000 wedding and reception venues; plan your wedding; chat to other brides about their experiences and ask for advice from Aunt Betti our agony aunt. If your guests are online, too, we will even help you set up a wedding website to share details and photos with your family and friends.

Our extensive online content on every aspect of weddings and special occasions is now complemented by our range of books covering every aspect of planning a wedding, for everyone involved. Titles include the complete *Wedding Planner; How to Write a Wedding Speech, Jokes, Toasts and One Liners for Wedding Speeches, The Best Man's Wedding, Men at Weddings* and *The Wedding Book of Calm.*

Confetti also offer:
Wedding and special occasion stationery – our stunning ranges include all the pieces you will need for all occasions, including Christenings, namings, anniversaries and birthday parties.
Wedding & party products – stocking everything you need from streamers to candles to cameras to cards to flowers to fireworks and, of course, confetti!

To find out more or to order your confetti gift book, party brochure or wedding stationery brochure, visit: www.confetti.co.uk
call: 0870 840 6060; email: info@confetti.co.uk
visit: Confetti, 80 Tottenham Court Road, London W1T 4TE
or Confetti, The Light, The Headrow, Leeds LS1 8TL